Five Steps to Financial Freedom

A Biblical Guide

Lindell G. Douglas, CFP ®

Lindell G. Douglas is registered with and securities are offered through Kovack Securities, Inc. Member FINRA/SIPC. 6451 N. Federal Highway, Suite 1201, Ft. Lauderdale, FL 33308 and (954) 782-4771. Investment Advisory services are offered through Kovack Advisors, Inc. LDA Wealth Management, Inc., is not affiliated with Kovack Securities, Inc. or Kovack Advisors, Inc.

PUBLISHED BY:

Yahweh's Anointed Publishing

Where your writing comes to life, one page at a time

Jamaica, W.I.

Scriptures used are referenced accordingly.

ISBN: 978-976-96709-6-9

Cover Designed created by: Geek Resource Centre

(geekjamaica@gmail.com)

Published by: Yahweh's Anointed Publishing

Tel: 876-549-0063/876-438-2256

Email: yahwehsanointedpublishing@gmail.com

Website: https://yapublishing.com

DEDICATION

This book is dedicated to all dreamers. Especially to Justin Joseph, Jordae Jo-Hannah, Jamie Jo-Helen, and Tyler Yosef. Unlock the Joseph inside of you and dream again.

CONTENTS

ABOUT THE AUTHOR

Lindell G. Douglas is a devoted Christian. He accepted the Lord as his savior and was called to be a Minister of the Gospel. He served as the leader of King's Chapel Men's Ministry (Hartford, CT), a member of the Missionary Board, as well as a Minister at Pioneer Community Church (Pembroke Pines, FL). He combines his secular knowledge of finances with his biblical knowledge of the scriptures to set the captives free.

He is a proud graduate of Kingston College, in Kingston, Jamaica. He earned a bachelor's degree in finance with honors from the University of Phoenix and was inducted into the Delta Mu Delta Honor Society. He further enhanced his knowledge by completing his course study for the prestigious CFP® designation, offered by the CFP Board of Standard, at the College of Financial Planning in Denver, CO.

Lindell is admired for his philanthropic initiatives, performance records, driving radical growth, and building a successful financial infrastructure for the organizations he is affiliated with. He is not one to sit by and wait for things to happen, he makes things happen-all the while, infusing the teams he leads with infectious energy and passion that empowers them to think big, set stretch goals, and pursue their goals with an intensity and focus, where anything but success is unthinkable.

When Lindell is not busy writing, fishing, conquering his opponents on the golf course, traveling to exotic destinations, trying different cuisines, engaging in philanthropic initiatives to ensure financially disadvantaged children get an education or removing financial bottlenecks for his clients, he can be found spending time with his wife and family, mostly cooking delicious recipes.

Lindell G. Douglas, CFP® LDA Wealth Management - 954-306-8668 or LGD@LDAWealth.com
www.ldawealth.com

Lindell G. Douglas is registered with and securities are offered through Kovack Securities, Inc. Member FINRA/SIPC. 6451 N. Federal Highway, Suite 1201, Ft. Lauderdale, FL 33308 and (954) 782-4771. Investment Advisory services are offered through Kovack Advisors, Inc. LDA Wealth Management, Inc., is not affiliated with Kovack Securities, Inc. or Kovack Advisors, Inc.

ACKNOWLEDGMENTS

I want to thank my wife Marsha Marie Douglas for her constant encouragement throughout the preparation of this book. To my kids- thank you for allowing me to learn what unconditional love is.

I am grateful to Pastor Kimola Brown-Lowe and my Church family at Worship & Faith International- Fort Lauderdale (WAFIF FL) for inspiring me to research and prepare this book.

Thanks to Reverend Dr. LeRoy Bailey Jr. from the First Baptist Church in Bloomfield Connecticut, for being my first teacher and mentor in the Word of God. I have learned so much from you.

To Bishop Michael Mitchell from Kings Chapel in Hartford Connecticut, you are a true example of a man that lives by faith- I admire you.

Mr. Charles Watkins Esq., of Pioneer Community Church, thank you for believing in me, even when I did not believe in myself. Charles encouraged me to buy my first house in Florida, at a time when I thought I could not afford such luxury.

Gary Wallace, you have taught me more about financial wisdom than you will ever know.

Donat Grant, you are a true example of a Humanitarian- I admire your heart and dedication to those who are sick, grieving, or in distress.

To my mom- Adelaid Miller Douglas, you never buckled under pressure and always kept your household open to anyone who needed help. You showed me what survival means- even when life gave you lemons, you made lemonade.

Finally, to God, our great Creator and Father- thank you Lord for allowing me the opportunity to walk in your light.

Let's rise and conquer!

PREFACE

Energy & Matter

There are two major elements in this world – ENERGY & MATTER.

The birds use the wind to fly, by pushing down on the wind and flying on top of it. Plants need the sun, carbon dioxide, and water to survive. Both the birds and plants use energy to be fruitful and constantly turn energy into matter to survive and thrive. How can we use energy to survive and thrive?

In John 15:5 Jesus says "*I am the vine: you are the branches. If you remain in me, and I in you. You will bear much fruit; apart from me you can do nothing*"[1].

We as children of God must constantly walk in the spirit and stay connected to the source, so we can produce much fruit. We need matter to survive in this world. We must turn our energy into matter without becoming materialistic.

It does not only take money to make money, but it does take energy to makc matter. Ecclesiastes 10:19 states, "*A feast is made for laughter, wine makes life merry, and money is the answer for everything*"[2]. Money is a very important commodity on this earth. God did not create money; therefore, it has no seed. However, it is an important medium of exchange and a legal tender in

[1] New International Version (NIV) Bible, 2009, John 15:5

[2] New International Version (NIV) Bible, 2009, Ecclesiastes 10:19

this material world.

Tap into a Wonderful Promise

Galatians 3:29 states *"If you belong to Christ, then you are Abraham's seed, and heirs according to the promise."* What are the promises to Abraham that we are heirs to? Let us look at God's promise to Abraham.

Genesis 12- Abraham's Blessing

1. Make you into a great nation
2. Bless you
3. Bless those who bless you & curse those who curse you
4. People on the earth will be blessed through you
5. Make your name great, you will be a blessing

The above is an awesome promise from God, and we need to rise-up and live-up to the promise. God told Abraham, *"I will make you into a great nation"* therefore I know my children, grandchildren, great grandchildren, and generations to come, are blessed and I must do some legacy planning (We will discuss this further in Step 5).

I AM Blessed

Everyone who does business with me, and we are mutually bonded is blessed. Anyone who seeks to hurt me without a cause is doomed to failure. If the people on Earth are blessed through me, then how am I living my life to be a blessing? Am I helping to spread the Gospel? What does my checkbook tell me about how I am living? What tangible benefits am I making to society? And finally, is my name great? What about my credit worthiness? Do I pay my bills on time? Am I living with good character and integrity? Am I avoiding debts at all costs?

Ephesians 1:3-5, states "*Blessed be the God and Father of our Lord Jesus Christ, who hath blessed us with all spiritual blessings in heavenly places in Christ: according as he hath chosen us in him before the foundation of the world, that we should be holy and without blame before him in love: having predestinated us unto the adoption of children by Jesus Christ to himself, according to the good pleasure of his will*"[3]. God has chosen us in Him before the foundation of the world. We were conceived in the mind of God before the world was created.

We plan for our children before they are born. We buy a crib, set up the room, etc. It's in the same manner that God knew us before the world was created, He must have made plans for our life, livelihood, dreams, goals, etc. In fact, he has blessed us with all spiritual gifts. Now we must turn our spiritual gifts into matter to

[3] New International Version (NIV) Bible, 2009, Ephesians 1:3-5

survive on earth.

1 Corinthians 2:9-16 states "*However, as it is written: "What no eye has seen, what no ear has heard, and what no human mind has conceived"—the things God has prepared for those who love him—these are the things God has revealed to us by his Spirit. The Spirit searches all things, even the deep things of God. For who knows a person's thoughts except for their own spirit within them? In the same way, no one knows the thoughts of God except the Spirit of God. What we have received is not the spirit of the world, but the Spirit who is from God, so that we may understand what God has freely given us. This is what we speak, not in words taught us by human wisdom but in words taught by the Spirit, explaining spiritual realities with Spirit-taught words. The person without the Spirit does not accept the things that come from the Spirit of God but considers them foolishness and cannot understand them because they are discerned only through the Spirit. The person with the Spirit makes judgments about all things, but such a person is not subject to merely human judgments, for, "Who has known the mind of the Lord so as to instruct him?" But we have the mind of Christ*"[4].

God reveals the mystery of the universe, to those who are connected through his Spirit. Therefore, we must ask the Spirit to give us insights, and wisdom, open our eyes to see and set divine appointments for us.

---

[4] New International Version (NIV) Bible, 2009, 1 Corinthians 2:9-16

Spiritual Warfare

Matthew 18:18-20 states *"Truly I tell you, whatever you bind on earth will be bound in heaven, and whatever you loose on earth will be loosed in heaven. "Again, truly I tell you that if two of you on earth agree about anything they ask for, it will be done for them by my Father in heaven. For where two or three gather in my name, there am I with them."* [5]

The first time I read this scripture I thought, surely this is a misprint. God would never give a man this much power until I understood who we are. It is important to have a consensus and surround yourself with like-minded persons, with whom you can pray with about your dreams together and support each other. As the scripture above states, the Lord shows up in corporate prayer. As children of God who are walking under the Spirit of God and submitting ourselves to God's words, we have awesome powers to bind and lose things on this Earth. The question is, do you know who you are?

In a few sentenccs, write about who you are.

____

____

____

____

____

[5] New International Version (NIV) Bible, 2009, Matthew 18:18-20

STEP 1- DREAM

Dust off your dreams because it is your season for them to be fulfilled!

Joseph had a dream in Genesis 37:5. God speaks to us in dreams, hunches, and visions- that small gentle voice. We must open our minds to believe in our dreams. Have you noticed when you get a new vehicle, you start seeing the model vehicle everywhere? Your mind's eyes are now open to it and you will see it. Your eyes only show you what you program your brain through socialization to reveal to you.

Don't believe me? Ask three eyewitnesses about the detail of the same accident and you will get three similar but different stories. If you believe in your dreams, you will see solutions to accomplish them everywhere. Keep praying and walking in the spirit and watch God work for you.

There are some billionaires, millionaires, and professionals reading this right NOW. God is activating your dreams now.

What is your goal?

Write it below:

My goal is: -

____

____

____

____

____

365 Days Focus Prayer Guide

________AM ________Noon ________Sunset

Bring the dream back to God in prayer. Dedicate some of your prayer time to just listen as God speaks to your soul. Write down everything that drops into your spirit.

When you pray, ask God:

1. For insight
2. Help you to understand your uniqueness
3. Open your eyes
4. Your value propositions
5. Give thanks for small successes

Why should we pray when God knows all things?

Answer: Through prayer, we can:

1. Grow spiritually and transform our life
2. Find the scriptural references for our dreams and desires and bring it back to God
3. Make spiritual legislations and decrees
4. Conduct spiritual warfare on the enemy's plans and intercede for God's people.

Format for Effective Prayer

1. Worship & Praise God
2. Visualize and see Heaven on Earth (See yourself already having possession of the things you are praying about).
3. Ask for your petitions (Use scriptural reference to align to God's will).
4. Confess your sins and forgive others who sinned against you
5. Make decrees against evil, spiritual warfare, and intercession
6. Spend time "quieting the mind" and everything around you and LISTEN.
7. Write down any insights, inspirations, ideas you receive in your spirit
8. Evaluate with your spiritual leaders, what you received in your quiet time with God, against the scriptures and act on it immediately.

Write out your dreams and goals.

Dreams:

1. ____

____

2. ____

____

3. ____

____

4. ____

____

5. ____

____

Goals:

1. ____

____

2. ____

____

3. ____

____

4. ____

____

5. ____

____

Whatever dreams you had, large or small. This is the season for them to be fulfilled. So, dust off your dreams. Genesis 37: 5 states that "*Joseph had a dream, and when he told it to his brothers, they hated him all the more*"[6]. Joseph had a dream. God speak to us in dreams- he gives us ideas, visions, hunches, etc. We must open our minds to believe in our dreams.

However, be very careful with whom you share your dreams. Joseph's own brothers tried to kill him and kill his dream. Your dream must be protected from some family members, friends, and associates. The bigger the dream the bigger the opposition.

FAITH

Faith is necessary to carry our dreams to reality. Without faith, our dreams are dead on arrival. We must believe God and not act on our feelings. Faith is not based on emotions. Faith is action. James 2:26 states,

[6] New International Version (NIV) Bible, 2009, Genesis 37:5

"*as the body without the spirit is dead, so faith without works is dead*"[7]. We should not act on our feelings alone but on faith.

"Faith is the substance of things hoped for and the evidence of things not seen" (Hebrews 11:1). The Bible says *faith comes by hearing the words of God* (Romans 10; 17). On this journey, faith will be the glue that holds you to your dreams and goals. As you walk this road to your goals there will be numerous times that you will feel like quitting, especially when you are speaking the words of affirmation and nothing is happening. You will feel alone and discouraged. Understand that this is when you know it is working. If you are in darkness, you are at the right place. Do not quit. You are on the right path. Faith requires you to walk even when you do not see anything. Everything around you is falling apart. You are wondering to yourself if you got this right. You now have structure tension in your minds. Because your vision board, imagination, and affirmations are saying one thing but your reality is showing you something else. Whose report will you believe?

Your dreams and goals are bigger than your present reality and it will take faith to help you navigate the waters filled with vipers to get to your dreams. The seed must die in order to grow into a tree that will be loaded with fruits. During the death cycle, it is darkness. After the sprout comes up, the weeds come to kill it. Then during the growth phase, the insects and reptiles come to kill the young tree. When the blossoms come out, the

[7] New International Version (NIV) Bible, 2009, James 2:26

insects come to destroy them. The birds, insects, reptiles, and other animals come for the fruits. Understanding these phases will help you to protect your dreams and look out for these attacks.

Sometimes your dreams will not come to reality until you have developed the faith needed to fulfill them. King David had to kill a bear and a lion before he killed Goliath. By then, he had the faith, knowledge, uniqueness, and bravery to do anything for God's glory - and then he became a King. There is nothing wrong with taking small steps towards your dream until you have developed the faith to believe 100 percent in the fulfillment of your dreams. Like King David, kill your "bear" and your "lion" first before taking on the giant Goliath.

We have already established that God conceived us in His mind before the world was created. God always speaks of himself in the present tense. God is the great I AM, and He has adopted us as His sons and daughters. Therefore, we can walk into the throne room with boldness. I AM, is always used, not I WAS, or I WILL BE. The use of I AM refers to living in the now. It is important to see everything as you are already in possession of it because it was given to you before the foundation of the world. Your job is to search it out.

- [ ] Imagine yourself already in a position of

____

- [ ] Create a Vision Board

AFFIRMATIONS

☐ I am making $____________, spending $____________, investing $__________________ and saving $_________________ per year.

☐ I am giving ___________ of my income to further the Kingdom of God

Every day before bed and the first thing in the morning look at yourself in the mirror and repeat your affirmations. Make sure you are making eye contact with yourself. Visualize yourself already in possession of your dreams.

STEP 2- PLAN

> Habakkuk 2:2 "*and God answered me, and said, write the vision, and make it plain upon tablets, that he may run that readeth it. For the vision is yet for the appointment time, and it hasteth toward the end, and shall not lie: though it tarry, wait for it: because it will surely come, it will not delay*"[8].

Whatever solutions you get, write them down. Develop a plan and keep adjusting the plan as ideas are revealed to you. Also, acquire knowledge that is more specific to your dream and the wisdom necessary to make the dream a reality. A plan is a living document and it must be constantly updated as your situation changes. It is important for you to know that something happens when you write down your dreams – they come to life! But this is not automatic. There is much work to be done as you aim toward actualizing those dreams and goals. You must be the best sought-after person in your desired field.

Proverb 25:2 states, "*It is the glory of God to conceal a matter; to search out a matter is the glory of kings*". The plan is our way of searching it out. It is the Glory of God to conceal a matter. It is your job to search it out. If you do not make a plan, it means you did not plant. If you do not plant, your field will be taken over by weeds.

What is the status of your life right now? Is it overrun with weeds? ☐ Yes or ☐ No

---

[8] New International Version (NIV) Bible, 2009, Habakkuk 2:2

Judges 6: 11-16 states *"The angel of the LORD came and sat down under the oak in Ophrah that belonged to Joash the Abiezrite, where his son Gideon was threshing wheat in a winepress to keep it from the Midianites. When the angel of the LORD appeared to Gideon, he said, "The LORD is with you, mighty warrior." "Pardon me, my lord," Gideon replied, "but if the LORD is with us, why has all this happened to us? Where are all his wonders that our ancestors told us about when they said, 'Did not the LORD bring us up out of Egypt?' But now the LORD has abandoned us and given us into the hand of Midian." The LORD turned to him and said, "Go in the strength you have and save Israel out of Midian's hand. Am I not sending you?" "Pardon me, my lord," Gideon replied, "but how can I save Israel? My clan is the weakest in Manasseh, and I am the least in my family." The LORD answered, "I will be with you, and you will strike down all the Midianites, leaving none alive"*[9].

Gideon was not living up to the man that God created him to be. He was afraid of the Midianites. But the angel of the Lord activated what was already inside of him. Some of the insecurities we have in not doing a plan is like Gideon; we may feel the Lord is not with us. Where are all the wondrous acts we read about in the Bible? Why have we not seen them today? Where is God? As He abandoned us? Who am I? I am the poorest in my family. I do not have any formal education but people love my cooking. These insecurities are natural. Most of us have them but not until you write down the dreams for your life, believe you can and work towards them will

[9] New International Version (NIV) Bible, 2009, Judges 6:11-16

you actually fulfil them.

In Jerimiah 29:11, God talks about the plans He has for us. If God has a plan for us should not we have a plan for our lives based on His plans for us?

Let's start planning!

Start with who will help you

1. Center of influence:

   ____

   ____

2. Advisors:

   a. ____________________

   b. ____________________

   c. ____________________

   d. ____________________

3. Team:

   a. ____________________

   b. ____________________

   c. ____________________

   d. ____________________

4. Short-term goal (Less than 1 year- be specific):

5. Mid-term goal (2-5 years):

6. Long-term goal (5 years or more):

7. Knowledge you possess:

____

____

____

____

____

8. Unique gifts (burning desires to be the best):

____

____

____

____

9. SWOT- These are areas for you to pray about daily- starting at 6AM. Also to use in your self-talk, vision board, and affirmations.

I AM…

____

____

(Strengths)

____

____

(Weaknesses)

____-

____

(Opportunities)

____

____

(Threats)

Uniqueness

Joseph had a dream, but he also had the unique gift of interpreting dreams. This unique gift gave him the opportunity to become the overseer of Egypt (Genesis 41: 1-46). Discover your uniqueness, what are you good at? You may need to get specific knowledge through additional training. Become the best in your field. Thrive to dominate this space. This will be your value proposition. You must always let all stakeholders see the value you bring to the table. Mediocrity is not your friend. Be the BEST!

As Proverbs 22:29 states "*Do you see someone skilled in their work? They will serve before kings; they will not serve before officials of low rank.*"[10] Your uniqueness will open doors for you. Your uniqueness will do more for you than your education can do. It will make you a sought after person that everyone is looking to work with or work for. Acquire education but most of all develop your uniqueness. It will be vital to your success.

Monitor

Dream, Plan and Go.

Your plan must not be left on cruise control. Always monitor your progress on the journey to ensure you are still on the right track. On the journey to your goal, you will gain experience and therefore you may need to change course or fine-tune something. The monitoring step is another key to your success. Read over this chapter and note the following along the way.

What obstacles did you face?

____

____

What adjustment was made?

____

____

Obstacles will always come on the road to your goals.

[10] New International Version (NIV) Bible, 2009, Proverbs 22:29

Your plan should address the known ones and a contingency strategy in place to address the unknown ones.

Structure your plan in short term (less than 5 years), medium-term (5 years to 10 years), and long-term (over 10 years). Success in your short-term plan will help you to achieve your medium and long-term goals. You should note the obstacles you faced and how you overcame them. Make note of these obstacles and your action plans to conquer them, as you will see these again. The same obstacles in different forms will come up from time to time on your journey to your dream.

In the first three months, nothing will happen. The seed must die and germinate to be reborn. There will be structural tension in your mind. Your belief and reality are out of sorts. Sometimes you must take a few steps backward to propel forward. Like the motion of a swing on a child's playground. You may want to give up resolving the tension. In fact, things may be worse than where you started. The plan is working. Push through, you will get the solution to make the belief and reality get back into balance.

Luke 22:31-32 states: *"Simon, Simon, Satan has asked to sift all of you as wheat. But I have prayed for you Simon, that your faith may not fail. And when you have turned back, strengthen your brothers"*[11].

Noticed Jesus did not say Satan was not granted permission rather, he prayed for Simon. It is Satan's job to test every word of affirmation and declaration we

[11] New International Version (NIV) Bible, 2009, Luke 22:31-32

make. In sifting us, the chaff will separate from the wheat and pureness will be revealed. As we go through this sifting some will give up. Peter denied Christ three times as his words were tested but he was strengthened and went on to be very successful. Expect your dreams and goals to go through the fire, but be encouraged Christ has prayed for you.

Prioritize your goals and put them in order based on urgency. Deal with the most important ones first. Do not try to manage them all at the same time. Imagine you are an air traffic controller with one runway to land planes. You have several airplanes in the sky requesting to land. You would prioritize and land the planes based on needs. The plane with the lowest fuel and cannot circle, lands first. Then the one with a medical emergency on board, etc. in those order. Do the same with your goals. Do not burden yourself with trying to do all things immediately.

Develop a Financial Strategy or Business Plan. These are complicated documents therefore I suggest you seek professional assistance to design one specifically for your needs. Your Accountant, Certified Financial Planner, Banker, etc., may be a reliable resource to help you put together a good financial plan.

STEP 3- GO

Reap but do not eat the seed. What does that mean? Everything God created has a seed.

> Genesis 1:11 *"then God said, "Let the land produce vegetation: seed-bearing plants and trees on the land that bear fruit with seed in it, according to their various kinds"*[12].

It is a system; it reproduces on its own. God is not a slave to his creations; so whatever God gives you, make sure you set up a system that can run without you. We must have the mind of God. Money does not have a seed. It was created by man. In order to create a seed in your money you must invest it. You will need the income from the seed for the next stage of your growth cycle.

All wealth begins with being thrifty. Always pay yourself first. Always!!!

Remember these equations:

Eq1 - Income minus Savings equal Expenses

Eq 2 – Save 30%, Giveaway 10%, Invest In You 10%, Expenses 50%

If you practice any of these equations, you will be wealthy in no time.

In **equation 1**, take your net income to determine how much you want to save and minus that from your

---

[12] New International Version (NIV) Bible, 2009, Genesis 1:11

income first, then pay your bills. Use an automatic process tied to your payroll cycle to deduct the money and transfer it to your investments. It is important that you remove yourself from this process.

Equation 2:

Using your Gross Income, save 30%. This can be in your 401k or other retirement plan, Emergency Fund, Brokerage account, and regular Savings account. You determine the percentage for each of the above categories. For example, you decide to save 10% of your salary in your Emergency Fund until you have one year of expenses saved. Save 10% of your salary to your 401k or other retirement plan until your retirement date. Save 10% of your salary in your Brokerage Account to buy stocks, Mutual Funds, Electronic Trading Funds (ETF), Real Estate Investment Trusts (REITs), Bonds, CD's, or other investments. After meeting your Emergency Fund goal, you may want to save that 10% into a Savings Account to buy rental real estate, replace the refrigerator, or the car, household improvements, and so on.

> *This is not a solicitation or an offer to buy or sell any security. Investing involves risk, including loss of principal. Please consult your Financial Professional for additional information.*

Give away 10%. Help the poor, homeless, widows, orphans, and help spread the Gospel. We will cover this in more detail in Step 5 - Give.

Invest in You, 10%. Use this as your allowance to do

whatever you like. Whether it may be, vacation, a new watch, hobbies, training, or whatever else your heart desires.

Never let your expenses be more than 50% of your income. This may be hard for some people, however plan to get to this goal within a few years. Remember that in order to achieve anything great, you must sacrifice something.

What are you willing to sacrifice?

____

____

____

Put First Things First

The children of Israel came out of Egypt with cattle, herds of sheep, etc. (Exodus 12:31) but in Exodus 16: 31-32 they were complaining that they were hungry. Wait!!! What happens to the herd of animals that they had? They understood the principle that you can't eat the things that are there to sustain you. The herds gave them milk, and clothing and also used for offerings to the Lord.

In every stage of your growth, to get to your dreams, you will need a "war chest." Therefore, you must never eat your seed. Use the seed to build your war chest (a reserve of funds). The Lobster must shed his protective shell to grow and thus become vulnerable. It is during that stage you need the fruits from your seed to sustain you until you come through the process.

See below examples of Automatic Process

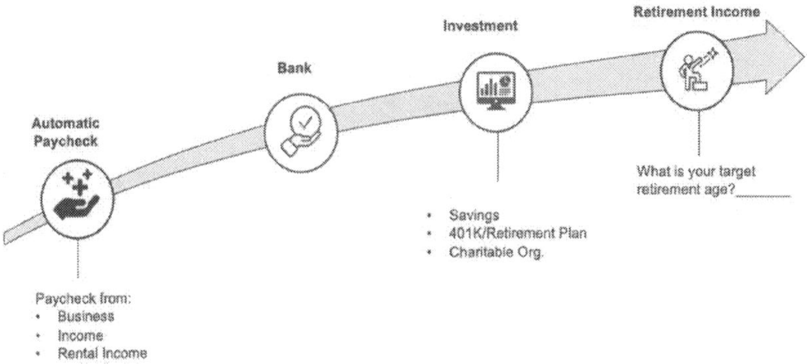

Picture 1: The Individual Process

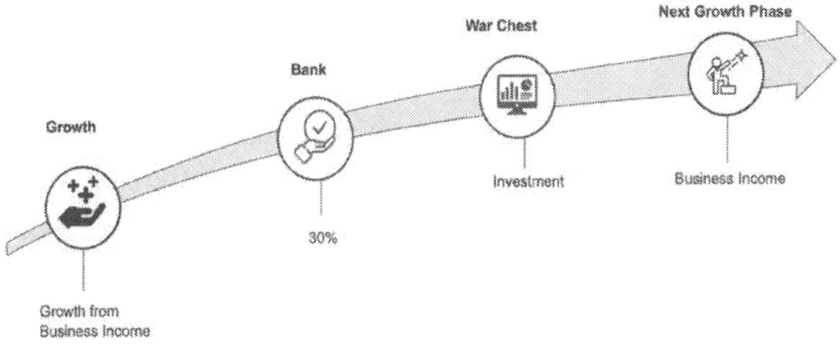

Picture 2: The Company Process

Set up automatic monthly payments from your bank account to your investment accounts. This process should be independent of you. The money flow is happening without you, and you don't feel it. If you are involved, chances are some months you will miss the payments and mess up the system.

What automatic processes are you setting up? Let's note it. I will automatically put away $_________________________monthly to savings.

Develop a Budget

First, take out your seed, then allot the rest of your income based on your desire and expenses. Money should move into savings and investments automatically. What are the benefits of budgeting you might ask? Simply put, a budget:

1. Allows you to prioritize your expenses and eliminate unnecessary ones.
2. Helps you to make sacrifices of what needs to be cut for you to reach your goals
3. Allows you to see your spending and understand exactly where your money is going.

Ask yourself the following:

1. Is my money going to what's important to me?

____

2. Is my spending helping me to reach my dreams and/or goals?

____

3. What am I willing to give up? What am I willing to cut from my budget so that I can reach my goals?

____

Let's closely examine where your income is going. Below, write in the monthly figure that you spend on the following:

1. Emergency Fund $________________________
2. Savings $________________________________
3. Investment $_____________________________
4. Charitable Savings $______________________
5. Mortgage/Rent $__________________________
6. Household Improvement $_________________
7. Light $___________________________________
8. Water $__________________________________
9. Cable/Internet $___________________________
10. Cell Phone $______________________________
11. Groceries $_______________________________
12. Lawn Care/Pool $__________________________
13. Pest Control $_____________________________

14. Car Payment $________________________

15. Car Replacement/Repair Fund $__________

16. Child Care/School $___________________

17. College Education Fund $______________

18. Life & Health Insurance $______________

19. Fuel/Gasoline $______________________

20. Auto Insurance $_____________________

Debt

21. Student Loan $_______________________

22. Credit Cards $________________________

Indiscipline and procrastination are two things that can railroad your best plan. Without a plan, or failure to follow the planned methodically will result in your life being the same next year as it is this year. All changes start with a step. Do not let procrastination and indiscipline rob you of your dreams. My friend Bob got a vision for a great idea and he tested it and got a pattern for his idea. He did nothing with it for years until someone called and offered him $100,000 for his pattern. He sold it for $100,000 and the buyer of the pattern turned his idea into a billion-dollar business. How many of us got ideas and did nothing and watched someone else take our ideas to market and become wealthy?

Focus

The birds don't have difficulties flying and the plants flourish "eating" the sun. You don't have to cheat, commit sexually immoral acts, etc. to be successful if you abide in God and watch Him work. We must be steadfast and don't recognize failure (Luke 18:1-8). In the referenced scripture, notice that the judge refused to grant justice to the widow but she was steadfast and didn't give up until she got justice. It doesn't matter how old you are (Joel 2) - NEVER GIVE UP on God and believe in yourself. Encourage yourself through positive self-talk. Nothing bad happens to you- everything happens for you (Romans 8:28). It may sound cliché but a bad situation can turn in your favor if you do not give up.

Dust off your dreams, write a plan, track and monitor your plan.

Build NERVES OF STEEL

1. Change the way you speak
2. Stay focused on your plan
3. Read it daily- mornings and at nights
4. Let it become a burning desire
5. Quit talking about what you want. (Live In the NOW, see yourself already in possession of it).
6. Always make a decision to act, and not act on your feelings.

7. Self-talk- Talk to yourself (Get your heart, soul, & mind aligned).
8. Be a better friend to yourself (do this – maintain eye contact and every day say I love you to yourself).
9. Choose to have faith in your abilities, but more importantly have faith in God.
10. Memorize the plan

Tricks of the enemy that prevents us from Succeeding

1. Jump up in church but there is nothing behind it. No fruits. What did Pharaoh say to the children of Israel? He told them to "Worship in the land". He wants us to worship when we are still in bondage, so we are not effective for the Kingdom of God on this Earth
2. The Family Unit is disjointed- We worship but the family is not there so the power of the family unit is diluted
3. Worship but we have no offering. We cannot make any impact for the Kingdom of God upon the Earth because the expenses to operate the church still require payment in money.

Let's break this cycle and change energy into matter

and change this world for Christ!!!

It is important that you read this book and commit it to understanding. If not, your joy about this good news will be short-lived.

Faith is fundamental for you to see success. If you allow discouragement and lack of self-worth to take root, you will not see your dreams materialize. In reaching my dreams, at first, I had moments of self-doubt and discouragement. Especially when making financial sacrifices and seeing others going out to eat and have a good time and my budget could not afford it. But always remember, fruits are ripened at different times, even though they might be on the same vine.

Picture 3: We all ripe at different times

So don't be discouraged that someone else is doing great and you are not. It's just not your season yet- be patient your time is coming.

You do not need shortcuts to succeed in God's plan. Do not let the cares of the world and the deceitfulness of riches ensnare you. What God has for you is so much better than all the riches of this world, and it comes without any sorrows. The key to judging those who fully got this message is the production of fruits. Some will see 100 percent of the fulfillment of their goals in the next 12 months. Others 60 percent and others 30 percent.

Your faith and action will determine your ultimate success.

STEP 4- DIVERSIFICATION

Ecclesiastes 11:2 states *"Invest in seven ventures, yes, in eight; you do not know what disaster may come upon the land"*[13]. Joseph spoke about the seven good years and seven bad. The Proverb 31 woman invested in several ventures. Taking advantage of the seasons and economic cycles- Boom, Decline, Recession, and Recovery; then Boom again.

Diversification is an important concept to implement in a successful investment strategy. Try to diversify your investment holdings in at least seven different things. The Proverb 31 woman was wise to this concept. She had different lines of business for the seasons. She dealt in Global trade. She ran her household and several successful business ventures. She manufactured garments of wool and flax, farming, and winemaking, took care of the poor, manufactured carpet and tapestry, made linen garments, and sold girdles to merchants.

Matthew 25: 14-30 speaks about the parable of talent. A lack of knowledge about investments and fear of loss is not an excuse not to produce fruits from investments and fear of loss is not an excuse not to produce fruits from what God has given us. If you are unable to design the investment strategy for yourself like the Proverb 31 woman, then at least consult with financial professionals to help you manage it.

[13] New International Version (NIV) Bible, 2009, Ecclesiastes 11:2

Investment Opportunities are always around us

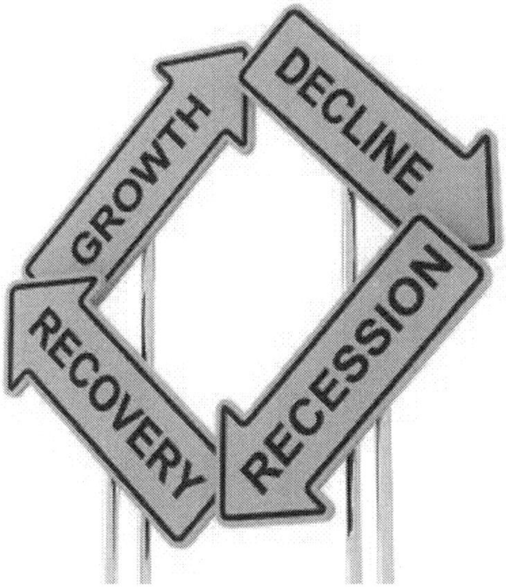

Picture 4: The Economic Cycle

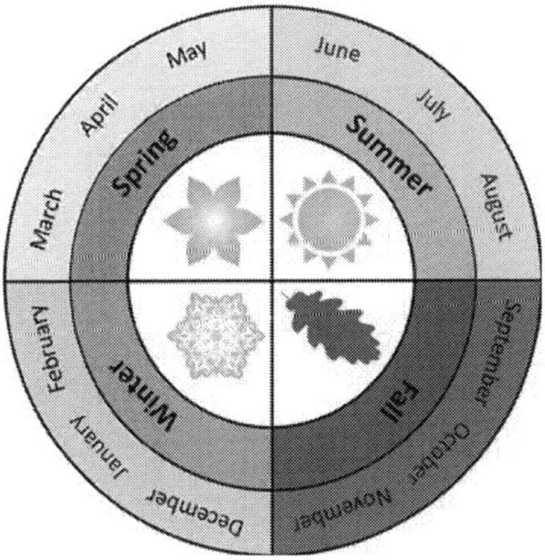

Picture 5- The Four Seasons

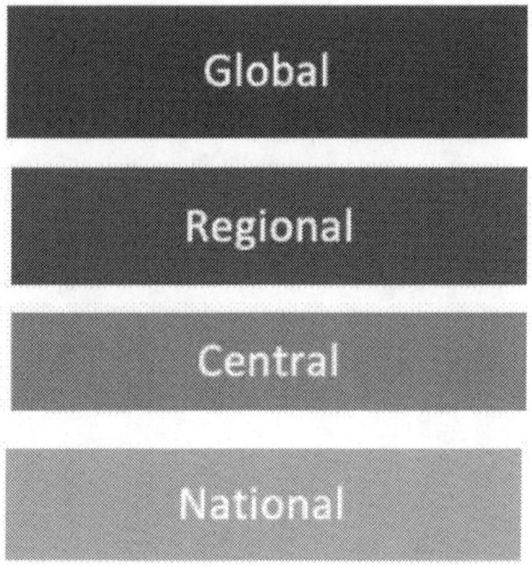

Picture 6- The Regions

1. How will you diversify your investments?

____

____

____

____

2. How will you take your dreams globally?

____

____

____

____

3. How will you take advantage of the four seasons?

____

____

____

____

Determination

Jose was poor growing up in the inner city of Kingston, Jamaica. His entire family migrated to the United States. The adjustment was not easy for them and they struggled financially. Jose's dad could not find a suitable permanent job and the family's financial affairs were in total disarray.

Jose determined in his mind at a young age he was not going to be poor and developed a burning desire to be successful at all costs. Jose was not the best student in high school. He barely maintained a C average. He was not voted best student or most aspiring student at graduation. He graduated (barely) and enrolled in the local university. Again, he struggled to excel but in his mind, he was not going to give up. He was going to make it.

He graduated from the University, found a job, and immediately enrolled to do his MBA. He was getting by with pure determination. However, in the workplace, he excelled. His resilience and determination to be the best have found a home at ZXY Technologies Inc. After two years, he earned his MBA and was promoted. He was making six figures now and his family was happy he was doing well.

He saw this beautiful girl at church and prayed about her. God told him in a vision she was his wife. One day he got the courage to go up to her and told her what God said. She laughed at him and said, "Well, God didn't tell me anything about that, so until He tells me that, please leave me alone."

This young woman was studying to be a Pharmacist. Let us call her Sally. Sally's family is also from Jamaica. Her parents are friends with Jose's parents and they all attended the same church. She was five years younger than Jose, and had no interest in him. Somehow Jose's vision, determination, resilience, and a burning desire for her convinced Sally to marry him. With their combined income, they were a rising star, "a power couple".

Jose and Sally sat down and planned their future life together. They set the date they wanted to retire, and they developed a budget. They put away money for retirement, emergencies, savings, Investments, and to help their future children pay for college education and not be loaded down with student loan debts like they were. They decided they would pool their respective salaries in a joint account. Then each one will have the same monthly allowance to a single checking account in their name to do whatever they desire without the other one asking questions. They decided on the amount they would save automatically every month to their Emergency Fund, Investment Account, 401k, Vacation Club, Car Replacement/ Repair Savings Account, General Savings, and church.

They also developed a Savings/Investment Policy Statement for the family for each one to abide by. It includes the following:

- The risk they are willing to take with the family funds.
- The type of investments they can purchase.
- Money can't be withdrawn from any of the accounts for any reason until their goal is reached.
- Who would be primarily responsible for managing the account.
- They would never buy two new cars at the same time just in case something goes wrong in their financial life so they are not carrying too much debt.
- They would take lunch to work Monday to Thursday and save that money into their vacation club.
- They would wait to fully furnish and decorate their home until their Savings Account was at $100,000.

- Any expense over $1,000 require mutual consent before purchase.
- They would give 15 percent of their income to Charity. This includes friends and relatives calling for money and when the limit is exhausted. It is exhausted for the month unless they can cut something else from their budget to do more.
- They will avoid debt at all costs and only use credit cards within the monthly budget and pay the balance off each month.

They were serious about their financial future and their desire to be successful. Their investment portfolio was doing great. They were happy with the sacrifices they made and two sons were added to the family. A nuclear family rising out of poverty to make a difference in the world.

Jose had invested heavily into technology funds, as he was familiar with that sector and then the technology bubble burst. It looked like they had lost everything, as 50 percent of their investment was gone. The family made a decision to hire a professional to help them weather the storm. Some 20 years later with their burning desire for success, financial acumen, and professional help, they are worth over 10 million dollars. With $7,000,000 in liquid investments.

The Bible says, one can put a thousand to flight but two

can put 10,000 to flight (Psalm 133:1). This shows the power of a unified family. Jose and Sally united their marriage in every area of their lives. Some couples have separate financial lives and that may work for them because of other constraints and trust issues. However, the power of a united couple must never be overlooked. The family unit can be such a powerful force no wonder the world tries to destroy the family at every turn. The family was doing well but lacked one thing, a diversified investment portfolio.

Global Mindset

Employ diversification in everything. It is important to try to understand different cultures, languages, regions, and countries. The World is global and so your mindset must be global. Think about how you can get your dream into every corner of this world. When God gives you a vision it is BIG. Do not just cater to your hometown, your culture, your language, etc. Go out of your comfort zone and influence the World.

STEP 5- GIVE

Don't Just Live for Yourself & Family

Remember the poor, widows, orphans, and the church. One of my favorite scriptures is Proverb 19:17 which states: "*Whoever is kind to the poor lends to the LORD, and he will reward them for what they have done*"[14]. The scriptures are filled with references of how God wants us to live and represent Him as an ambassador on this earth. One will never understand the joy of life until one live a life of charity.

A hand that is clenched cannot receive. Giving to the poor is a form of thanksgiving to God. This is putting your words into action, Sharing is caring! Some of the richest people in the world are some of the biggest givers. Sowing and reaping is a universal law. You cannot bypass it as much as you cannot bypass the law of gravity. Cornelius's name came up before God because of a life of charity (Acts 10: 2-6).

There is no one I want to lend to more than the Lord. He is the biggest giver and I want Him to always see me as someone He can trust with His knowledge, wisdom and financial resources. The more I give, the more the Lord gives to me. Therefore, I can never run out of resources. Luke 6:38 clearly states "give and it shall be given unto you. The measure that you use to give, is the same measure that people will use to give to you. So, in essence, I determine the measure of my success by the measure I use to give. Some people can give, but do not.

[14] New International Version (NIV) Bible, 2009, Proverb 19:17

Some people can give, but just don't remember to give, while others make a habit of giving. They set up a system to give and it is now a lifestyle.

Legacy

One of the best ways to give is to ensure you are leaving a legacy for a generation unknown to you. The blessing of Abraham should be your guide. It is important to make sure your name is remembered for generations.

Proverbs 13:22 states, *"A good person leaves an inheritance for their children's children, but a sinner's wealth is stored up for the righteous".*[15] Gifting your wealth at death to the next generation is one way to ensure your legacy, you can control how it is done to make sure their innovativeness, and creativity are not stifled by sudden wealth. Setting various Trusts can help you accomplish this goal. Your legacy may include a gift to your alumni, religious organizations, and or other charitable organizations you cared about and want your name to be established there.

What is a Trust?

____

____

____

[15] New International Version (NIV) Bible, 2009, Proverb 19:17

Estate Planning

The CFP Board of Standards defines Estate planning as the legal planning that helps you control who will inherit your money and property, and who can make medical and financial decisions on your behalf if you are unable to do so yourself.

Charitable giving should be a part of your estate plan. There are several benefits to set up charitable giving and it shows where your heart is concerning the things of God. You can leave money to Charity in a:

- Will (A will is a legal instrumental used to establish a beneficiary on all properties without a named heir)
- Donate your Individual Retirement Account (IRA) to a Charity.
- Establish a Community Foundation
- Give Your Property
- Gift Appreciated Stock
- Create a Charitable Remainder Trust
- Use Life Insurance or a Charitable Gift Rider

There are numerous tax benefits to the above. Please consult with a financial and estate professional for more detailed information.

Be Shrewd

Luke 16: 1-13 *"Jesus told his disciples: "There was a
rich man whose manager was accused of wasting his
possessions.* **2** *So he called him in and asked him, 'What
is this I hear about you? Give an account of your
management, because you cannot be manager any
longer.'* **3** *"The manager said to himself, 'What shall I do
now? My master is taking away my job. I'm not strong
enough to dig, and I'm ashamed to beg—* **4** *I know what
I'll do so that, when I lose my job here, people will
welcome me into their houses.'* **5** *"So he called in each one
of his master's debtors. He asked the first, 'How much
do you owe my master?'* **6** *"'Nine hundred gallons[a] of
olive oil,' he replied. "The manager told him, 'Take your
bill, sit down quickly, and make it four hundred and
fifty.'* **7** *"Then he asked the second, 'And how much do
you owe?' 'A thousand bushels[b] of wheat,' he replied.
"He told him, 'Take your bill and make it eight hundred.'*
8 *"The master commended the dishonest manager
because he had acted shrewdly. For the people of this
world are more shrewd in dealing with their own kind
than are the people of the light.* **9** *I tell you, use worldly
wealth to gain friends for yourselves, so that when it is
gone, you will be welcomed into eternal dwellings.*
10 *"Whoever can be trusted with very little can also be
trusted with much, and whoever is dishonest with very
little will also be dishonest with much.* **11** *So if you have
not been trustworthy in handling worldly wealth, who
will trust you with true riches?* **12** *And if you have not
been trustworthy with someone else's property, who will
give you property of your own?* **13** *"No one can serve two
masters. Either you will hate the one and love the other,*

or you will be devoted to the one and despise the other. You cannot serve both God and money."

The above scripture teaches of a shrewd but dishonest manager. It is good to be shrewd but not dishonest. Do not give away what doesn't belong to you; rather be astute and sound in judgment. People may use their worldly wealth to gain friends. Have you ever noticed who anyone looks for in a group picture of them self and friends? Yes, themselves.

- It is important to celebrate people – remember their birthdays, anniversaries, favorite hobbies, etc.
- Let people be in debt to you.
- Become a resource broker
- Serve humanity with your talent and treasure

I am serving humanity by giving to:

1. ________________________________
2. ________________________________

Let's dust off our dreams and put in a process to achieve!

Thank You
YOUR FAITH AND ACTION WILL
DETERMINE YOUR ULTIMATE SUCCESS

Lindell G. Douglas, CFP®

lgd@ldawealth.com

www.ldawealth.com

Officc - 954-306-8688

Lindell G. Douglas is registered with and securities are offered through Kovack Securities, Inc. Member FINRA/SIPC. 6451 N. Federal Highway, Suite 1201, Ft. Lauderdale, FL 33308 and (954) 782-4771. Investment Advisory services are offered through Kovack Advisors, Inc. LDA Wealth Management, Inc is not affiliated with Kovack Securities, Inc. or Kovack Advisors, Inc.

Made in the USA
Columbia, SC
18 February 2023

12333347R00030